Annie Books Book Six: Taming Tommy's Tantrums

Annie Books Series © by Michelle Fattig

Experience Asperger's Syndrome and Attention Deficits Through the Eyes of a Child
www.anniebooks.com

A Windy Day with Annie

A Prairie Day with Annie

Bully-Be-Gone with Annie

Viva Le Resistance!

Calming the Stormy Days with Annie

Taming Tommy's Tantrums

Coming soon to Annie Books

Making Friends and Keeping Them with Annie

Learning to be Nice with Annie

Stopping the Blurting Days with Annie

Managing the Distracto-Days with Annie

Annie Books Book Six: Taming Tommy's Tantrums

Annie Books Book Six: Taming Tommy's Tantrums

Written by Michelle Fattig

(Featured on Autism One Radio with Rhonda Brunett, "Unlocking the Door to Autism.")

Pictures by Josh Fattig

(Featured on Global Talk Radio: Living with Asperger's Syndrome-A Teen's Perspective)

"A Prairie Day with Annie: It's a very charming, well-written book and I'm sure it will help countless children and families dealing with ADD and Asperger's Syndrome. I wish you the best of luck and success with your valuable work." Lindsay Miller, Readers Digest

"...Annie struggles to remember life's many details and finds it difficult to fit in." --Kirkus Discoveries on A Prairie Day with Annie: Experience Attention Deficits Through the Eyes of a Child

"A Prairie Day with Annie, is enjoyable and easy to read, while wonderfully illustrating the creative mind, frustrating experiences, and hopeful possibilities of one who has ADD." Paul Chleborad, Psy.D., MA, MFCT, Licensed Psychologist

"Conversationally and conspiratorially, Annie addresses the reader..." --Kirkus Discoveries A Windy Day with Annie

Annie Books Book Six: Taming Tommy's Tantrums

Annie Books Book Six: Taming Tommy's Tantrums

Taming Tommy's Tantrums

by Michelle Fattig, Ed.S.

pictures by Josh Fattig

Annie Books©

Flower by the Water Publishing

Genoa, NE

Annie Books Book Six: Taming Tommy's Tantrums

This book is dedicated

to my wonderful husband,

amazing children,

and our family.

 Published in the United States by Flower by the Water Publishing.

Fattig, Michelle. Taming Tommy's Tantrums / Michelle Fattig ; Illustrated by Josh Fattig.

"Annie Books" SUMMARY: In his own words, a young boy describes his feelings and emotions about living with Asperger's Syndrome and Attention Deficit Disorder, the frustration in our brains, and how to feel better.

ISBN 978-0-9795805-7-4(pbk)

Manufactured in the United States of America.

Michelle and Josh have
Asperger's Syndrome
and Attention Deficit Disorders.
They use their unique insight
and experience to fight crime, battle evil,
promote world peace,
and to create this humorous,
yet meaningful story of a child
experiencing the challenges of
Asperger's Syndrome and Attention
Deficit Disorder.

Annie Books Book Six: Taming Tommy's Tantrums

Annie Books Book Six: Taming Tommy's Tantrums

Taming Tommy's Tantrums

"Mom! Mom! Mom! Mom! Mom! Mom!" Tommy yelled, racing into the room excitedly.

"Tommy, please! Give me a second to think!" His mother replied, rubbing her temples in irritation.

Tommy ducked his head, kicked a chair, and scowled.

"Honestly Tommy, pick up that chair and fix your face!"

"Fix my face huh," Tommy muttered as he straightened the chair.

"How about I fix *your* face!"

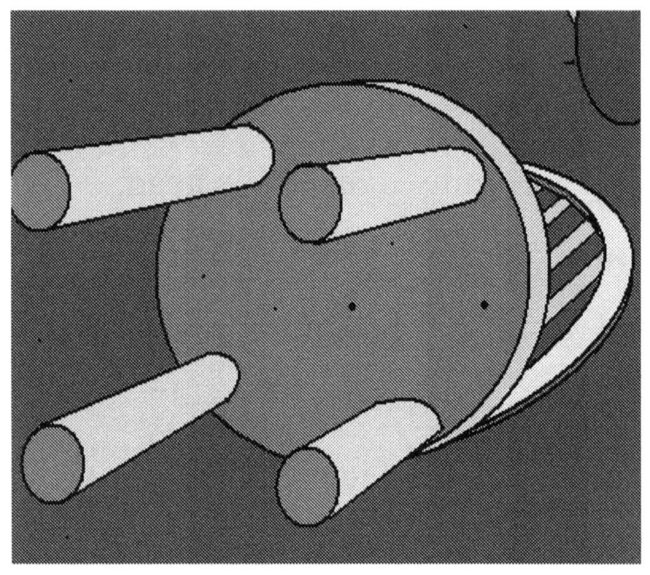

"What was that young man?"

"Nothing," Tommy snarled, stomping off to his room.

Tommy flew into his room, slammed the door, looked around, took a deep breath, and his eyes welled up with tears.

"Fix your face Tommy, honestly Tommy, what is your problem Tommy, stop looking at me Tommy, look at me Tommy, stop picking Tommy," he muttered irritably to himself.

With slumped shoulders, and a suspicious burning behind his eyes and in his nose, Tommy opened his closet door.

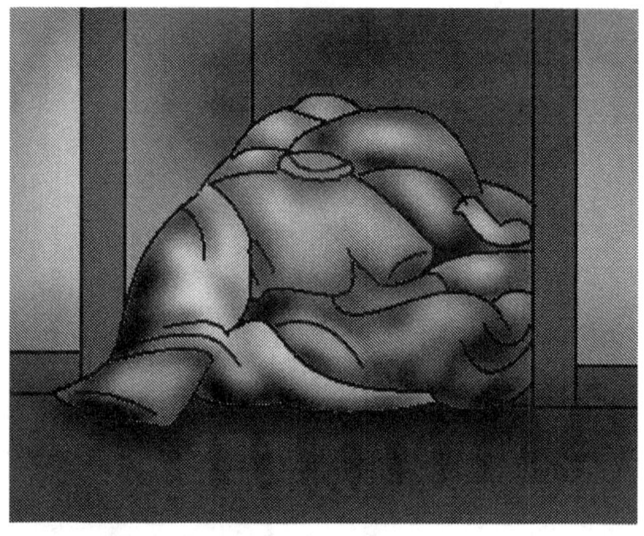

He kicked at the dirty clothes piled inside, "Pick up your clothes Tommy, wash your face Tommy, brush your teeth Tommy.

Stop talking Tommy, stop tipping your chair Tommy…"

"Tommy this, Tommy that," he continued, but this time the irritability was gone, and was replaced with a sniff and a large lump in his throat.

"Miss Timpkins said, if we play in her little *group*, we would make *friends*, and be *happy,* and blah, blah, blah," Tommy wiped at his nose, "Yeah right. Who would ever want to be good old *Tommy's* friend? No one!"

Tommy burrowed deep into his closet, and pulled the pile of clothes over himself.

I hate having Asperger's, he thought to himself.

When he was younger, Tommy had tried very hard to explain the "Tommy questions," but no one ever listened.

He would tell them the truth; he didn't *know* why.

But, *OH NO*, "I don't know isn't an answer Tommy." "You need to think about it Tommy."

"Maybe you can think about it while you miss PE Tommy."

"Tommy should not get recess for a week if he can't give a better answer," The many, *many* lectures he had heard, echoed through his thoughts, over and over and over…

But I *don't* know, Tommy thought to himself.

I *don't* know why I kicked Jamie, after Cathy laughed at me for missing the ball.

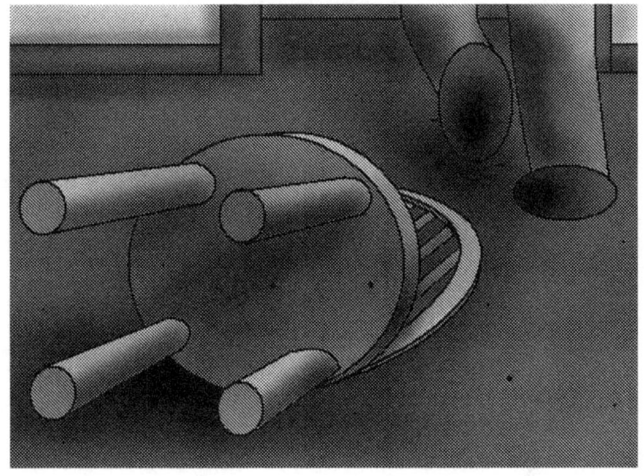

I don't know why I knocked the chair over, when I forgot the paper Mrs. Jansen reminded me to turn in.

I had it done; I just don't know what happened to it!

I don't know why I can't look at the teacher when she is talking to me.

I don't know why I jump or hit people who touch me unexpectedly.

I don't know why loud noises make me want to cover my ears or make me shove things off my desk.

I don't know why the cafeteria makes my stomach hurt, and I can't eat my lunch.

"You just sit right there young man," the lunch ladies say, "You can just sit until you eat. Recess can wait."

Don't they know that if I sit and wait, I feel itchy all afternoon, and can't stop squirming?

I don't know why I hid under the chair when mom had all of those ladies over.

I don't know why, when Mrs. Meyer sat in the chair,

I growled all low in my throat, and grabbed her ankle like a claw.

I don't know why I told Miss Trailsley that her holiday lights were crooked, and it hurt my eyes to look at them.

I don't know why I can't just 'stop my mouth and listen for a change.'

Tommy shrugged deeper under the clothes pile, trying to drown out all of the lights in the room.

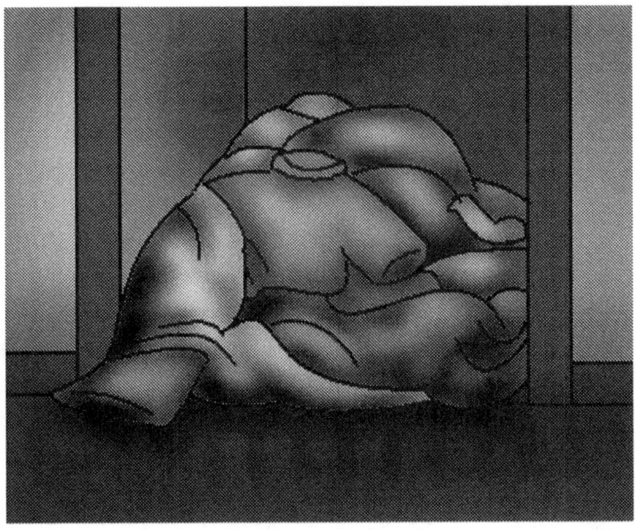

I don't know why I didn't shut the dumb lights off.

Tommy began absently picking at the scab on his finger.

He knew he wasn't supposed to pick, "Stop picking Tommy," but sometimes, he just couldn't help himself.

Scabs really bug Tommy.

They just shouldn't be there.

When Tommy gets worried, or anxious, or stressed, or mad, it is almost impossible *not* to pick, sometimes even when there isn't a scab to begin with!

Later in the evening, Tommy heard his father pull in the drive.

He heard the familiar humming of the engine stop.

He heard the creak of the door opening.

He heard the slam, and crunch, crunch, crunch of his dad's feet, as he walked across the driveway.

He heard the back door open, and slam shut.

Here we go, Tommy thought to himself.

He heard the all too familiar murmuring of his parents.

Now comes the 'Why can't you just,' lecture. "Why can't you just get along Tommy?" "Why can't you just entertain yourself Tommy?" "Why can't you just sit still Tommy?" "Why can't you keep your hands to yourself Tommy?"

"Why can't I just be like everyone else?" Tommy muttered

aloud, as he heard the door swing open.

"Hey kiddo," he heard his dad say, "Where are you, buddy?"

"In here," came the muffled reply.

"In where?"

"In here," Tommy said, shoving the clothes to the floor, and opening the closet door.

"Rough day?"

"Yeah."

"Want to talk about it?"

"No."

A brief silence hung in the room.

Then Tommy's Dad did something completely new.

He opened the closet door wider, shoved at the pile of clothes, and hunkered down beside Tommy.

With wide eyes, Tommy looked over at his dad.

The hangy up clothes were bunched around Dad's head and shoulders, sort of like a weird wig.

One pants leg was draped across his forehead, and a belt draped oddly around his neck, like a flat, deranged snake.

"So," Dad said, "rough morning equals a rough day, huh?"

Tommy looked at his dad in confusion.

"Don't think I noticed, did you?" Dad continued.

Still, a confused look was the only reply.

His dad cleared his throat, shifted his weight around a bit, blew upward to dislodge the pants leg, which only slid sideways, knocking Dad's hair askew.

"This morning your mom and I were in a hurry to get going, yeah?"

Tommy's head dropped, and he nodded.

"And you came flying at me, with your hands out, yelling, 'Hey Dad, Dad, Dad,' right?

"And I said that I was late, right?

"And you felt that feeling, right?" his father asked in a quiet voice.

Tommy felt very hot all of the sudden.

The top of his head felt all squeezy, and his stomach felt like he had just ridden over the top of the Ferris wheel.

Tommy hates this feeling.

He gets it when someone corrects him, or his schedule gets

changed, or there is a substitute teacher, or…

His thoughts were interrupted, as his dad continued, "That's why you kicked me, isn't it?"

Tommy swiped his hand at a shirt, "Stupid shirt."

Dad continued to stare straight ahead as he talked to Tommy, which helped.

Tommy doesn't feel the tight in his chest feeling as much, when he doesn't have to look at someone talking to him.

"You wanted my attention, and I was too busy to notice.

"That hurt your feelings and gave you the itchy-hot-squeezy-weird in the stomach feeling, yeah?"

Dad elbowed Tommy in the side a little.

Silence.

"Yeah?" Another little elbow jab.

Tommy, irritably replied, "Yeah, I guess."

"Tommy, I know that it is hard to talk about feelings. I also know that it is hard for you, when you try to make friends, or talk to someone, or ask for something, and it doesn't work out the way you had hoped."

No response.

"But you have to understand, that other people have routines and things to get done, and sometimes we don't realize that we have disappointed you," his dad said.

No response.

"Sometimes, you need to understand that it is up to you to tell us, in a nice way, that you need our attention."

Tommy shifted a little, "What do you mean?"

"Well, how about, instead of kicking me, you say something like, 'Dad, I need your attention right now,' and that will be my cue to look at you, ask you a specific question, and give you a hug?"

"No hugs!" Tommy practically shouted.

Chuckling, and ruffling Tommy's hair, his dad replied, "Okay, no hugs. But you can't blame me for trying to sneak that one in on you!"

His dad crawled forward, out of the closet, and stood, wiping at the dust bunnies on his pants, "Let's practice, shall we?"

"Practice makes perfect," Tommy grinned, knowing that if they didn't practice and prepare, he would never be able to remember if the itchy-hot-squeezy-weird in the stomach feeling, took over first!

We hoped you have enjoyed our *Taming Tommy's Tantrums*. For more Annie Books, please visit us at: www.anniebooks.com

Michelle, Josh, and Lilianne

Reaching the world, one book at a time!

For parents and educators…

Don't use the F word with me!

Hyper-reactive or Hypo-reactive to Stimuli
We need to understand and manage sensory overload and "under-load."
We can't be cured, but we can learn to cope!
By Michelle Fattig

What is fair?
Fair is not equal.
Fair is not treating everyone the same.
Fair is doing what needs to be done,
so that everyone gets what he or she needs.

To some, we appear to be odd, difficult to read, aloof, or unique, but we are really foundering in a world of unwritten rules in social interactions. We sometimes 'make up our mind' and it is almost impossible to sway us, or 'get us to understand' another's perspective. We may abruptly leave a conversation, sometimes in the middle of a sentence, and we may announce that we are 'never coming back!'

We are almost constantly at the mercy of our ever-fluctuating sensory reactions, with our emotional valve systems either fully open, or fully closed. We are rarely at an emotional calm, within our own person. We tend to have delayed response times, while we process information, and can have some difficulty organizing and retrieving thoughts, words, answers, or responses.

Emotions are a sensory issue, as much as taste, touch, sound, light, proprioception, or other more commonly included sensory issue. Emotions hit us like a sack of potatoes, we are able to relive memories in context with vivid mental images of acute detail, and usually those memories are distinctly negative in nature, a failure of some kind. We know we will 'fail' on any given day; it is simply a matter of when and how bad. All emotions are treated with some suspicion, with the distinct exception of anger.

Anger we know, anger we can see, anger we can trust. Joy is fleeting, and can be too overwhelming. Sadness is all encompassing and almost unbearable. When the valve is wide open, emotionally, sadness can be catatonic. When the valve is fully shut, emotionally, sadness is: numbness, hollowness, head pressure, and avoidance.

Compliments are a double-edged sword. Briefly, it leads to a warm feeling in our chest, and our faces feel flushed. Embarrassment is an enormous sensory overload issue, and we can become embarrassed at a comment, glance, or shrug. Embarrassment can sneak in through a compliment, correction, look, or other seemly innocuous gesture, leading us to a valve wide-open systems overload. It is acutely uncomfortable, and as we experience this, we tend to look for the emotion we can trust: anger.

What this may look like to those who are not on our team:

- Walking away in the middle of a conversation
- Storming off to our room
- Quitting a job, or being unable to go back
- Refusing to answer the phone or open the door
- Getting mad at a compliment, or shutting down and refusing to work or interact
- Tears or tantrums with little or no provocation
- Multiple moves or job changes
- Physical violence
- Avoidance
- Abruptly changing behavior
- Picking, tattling, arguing

Individually, if someone on our team is acting out, being difficult, having a tantrum, or becoming avoidant, rest assured that something in his or her environment, job, social interaction, classroom, or home is not meeting the definition of fair. Something is not being presented in such a way that he or she can understand, some trust issue has been broken, or other sensory overload is occurring.

Routine
If you change our routine unexpectedly, you will fling the emotional valve wide open or fully shut! Change is overwhelming to our sensory systems, and can be devastating. Change in the home, school, workplace, dinnertime, teachers, level of noise, crowded spaces, or invasion of personal space leads to high anxiety, frustration, and acting out or acting in.

Acting out: tantrums, hitting, kicking, swearing, yelling, giggling uncontrollably, loud voice, etc.

Acting in: withdrawal, quiet, stomachache, headache, crying, masking, etc.

Acter-outers tend to appear to be more defiant, difficult, oppositional, and take more risks

Acter-inners tend to have more physical symptoms, eating disorders, anxiety disorders, obsessive-compulsive issues, depression, and tend to be more vulnerable to abusive relationships

We have difficulty understanding or trusting facial expressions, body language, and social cues. Sometimes we have difficulty following a conversation or directions, give us prompts and visual cues. We have difficulty 'getting' jokes, sarcasm, or multiple meanings, explain it to us simply and with concrete examples.

Avoid abstracts! Saying, "Be nice," is too vague. Saying, "Listen to what the other person is saying, make one comment that is of a similar nature, and then you can talk about…" is concrete, we get the rules, and we can follow them! We have a distinct difficulty with reciprocal language. It might not occur to us that we should ask how someone's day is, or how his or her family is, because it isn't a functional part of our day. Understand that we don't often hang out in the break room, because we can't be social creatures, not because we don't want to be social creatures! As children, we want to make and keep friends; it is just that we don't know how!

What can you do?
As much as possible, 'listen' to the behavior. What is causing her to avoid school, friends, or food? What is causing him to fight at recess? Why does he get a stomachache everyday at lunchtime?

Interventions:

- Try to manage external levels of stimuli as much as possible (low levels of noise, movement, change, or other 'trigger')
- Try to ignore acting out unless specifically harmful to self, others, or property
- Consider a cuing system to identify and avoid 'triggers' before overload occurs
- Sensory outlets such as quiet, safe area (never use as a punishment)
- Fidgets, squishy toys, heavy blanket or vest, gum, chewies, crunchy or chewy foods, a tub of white rice, core strengthening seats, or other, which helps to calm psychomotor agitation or anxiety

- Break down tasks literally, visually, verbally, physically, realistically, and simply
- Remain calm and consistent
- Use schedules, journals, planners, and calendars
- Be aware of change in routine and prepare, practice and role play
- Create a crisis plan, in the event that sensory overload cannot be avoided, and stick to it
- Clothes, toothpaste, paper grain, Popsicle sticks, pencils, socks, tags, tastes, touch, smells can all cause sensory overload, be aware of needs, and address accordingly
- Teach, model, and practice social skills
- When all else fails, find humor in the situation and downplay any social blunder

Annie Books Book Six: Taming Tommy's Tantrums

To me, 'curing autism,' would be eliminating a fundamental part of my children and myself. 'Curing autism' is an understandably lofty goal, unless you consider the alternative, which is increasing understanding, awareness, and empathy in a less than tolerant society and promoting acceptance, empowerment, and diversity as the true meaning of fair.

Annie Books Book Six: Taming Tommy's Tantrums

For more by Josh Fattig, visit:

www.anniebooks.com

Annie Books Book Six: Taming Tommy's Tantrums

www.ingramcontent.com/pod-product-compliance
Lightning Source LLC
La Vergne TN
LVHW020658100826
845148LV00012B/2546

* 9 7 8 0 9 7 9 5 8 0 5 7 4 *